ALL ABOARD AMERICA

Oregon Trail

A Buddy Book
by
Sarah Tieck

ABDO
Publishing Company

VISIT US AT
www.abdopublishing.com

Published by ABDO Publishing Company, 8000 West 78th Street, Edina, Minnesota 55439.

Printed in the United States.

Contributing Editor: Michael P. Goecke
Graphic Design: Deborah Coldiron
Cover Photograph: North Wind Picture Archive
Interior Photographs/Illustrations: Library of Congress (page 22); North Wind Picture Archive (pages 5, 7, 9, 11, 13, 19); Photos.com (15, 22); Stockbyte (page 17)

Library of Congress Cataloging-in-Publication Data

Tieck, Sarah, 1976
    Oregon Trail / Sarah Tieck.
      p. cm. — (All aboard America)
    Includes bibliographical references and index.
    ISBN 978-1-59928-939-7
    1. Oregon National Historic Trail—Juvenile literature. 2. Pioneers—Oregon National Historic Trail—Social life and customs–Juvenile literature. 3. Frontier and pioneer life—West (U.S.)—Juvenile literature. 4. Overland journeys to the Pacific—Juvenile literature. I. Title.

F880.T55 2008
978'.02—dc22

                  2007027270

Table of Contents

CHAPTER 1

An Important Route

The Oregon Trail is a historic land route to what is now the western United States. This famous trail officially started in Independence, Missouri. It ended in Oregon City, Oregon.

In the 1800s, the West was not yet part of the United States. Mountain men, fur traders, and Native Americans lived on the unsettled land.

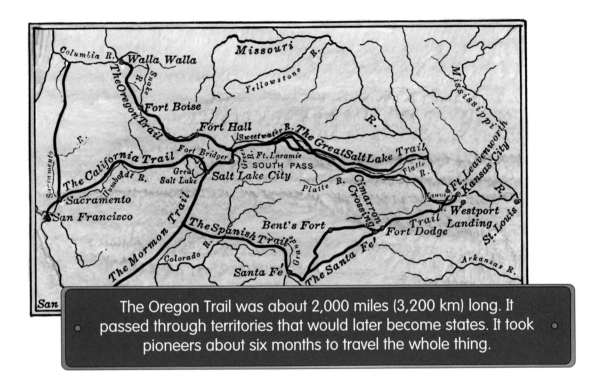

The Oregon Trail was about 2,000 miles (3,200 km) long. It passed through territories that would later become states. It took pioneers about six months to travel the whole thing.

The Oregon Trail allowed people to settle the West. Thousands of **pioneers** traveled in covered wagons across prairies and mountains.

In the 1800s, the eastern United States was very crowded. **Boosters** and posters advertised free land in the West. And in 1843, one of the first **wagon trains** reached Oregon.

People got excited. This excitement was called "Oregon Fever." From the 1840s to the 1860s, thousands of people used the Oregon Trail.

The trip along the Oregon Trail was very dangerous. Still, people took the risk. They wanted to claim the free land and start new lives.

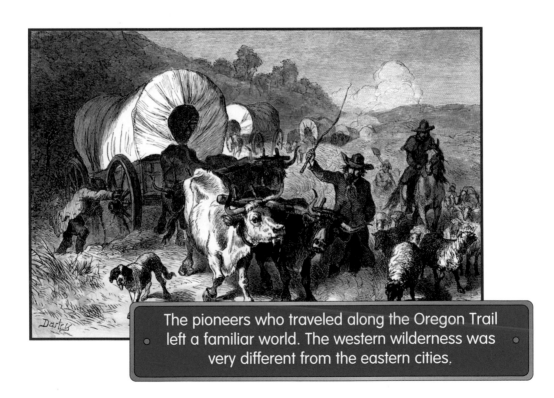

The pioneers who traveled along the Oregon Trail left a familiar world. The western wilderness was very different from the eastern cities.

There were many places to enter the Oregon Trail. But the official starting point was Independence, Missouri.

On the trail, there were few places to purchase supplies. So, **pioneers** bought covered wagons and supplies before starting their journey.

The wagons were small, so people packed only important items. Guidebooks explained what they would need for the journey. The lists included food, clothing, books, tools, pictures, and extra wagon parts.

A covered wagon cost about $110. The wagon box was about four feet (1 m) wide and ten feet (3 m) long.

Most **pioneers** traveled the Oregon Trail in **wagon trains**. Some large groups included more than 60 wagons. Others had just a few families. In groups, people could help each other when needed.

Teams of oxen pulled the loaded wagons through rough land. A wagon needed to be both strong and light to last the trip.

Wagon trains traveled in long lines. People often walked alongside their wagons. There was very little space to ride inside.

Often, a guide lead a group of wagons. When the guide was ready to start moving, he shouted, "Wagons, ho!"

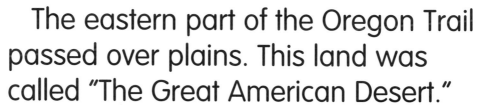

Crossing The Plains

The eastern part of the Oregon Trail passed over plains. This land was called "The Great American Desert."

The road was very rough. So, **wagon trains** traveled about 15 miles (24 km) each day.

It was important for groups to leave at the right time of year. If they left too early, there might not be enough grass for the oxen. Also, wagons could get stuck on the soggy, muddy prairie. If they left too late, they could get caught in winter storms.

Native Americans lived on the plains. Some people were afraid to meet them. Others traded with the tribes.

Sometimes pioneers stopped at forts. Forts had supplies, post offices, and medicine. Fort Laramie in present-day Wyoming, was one of the first army forts.

CHAPTER 5

Trail Challenges

Daily life brought many challenges for the **pioneers**. They traveled past wrecked wagons and abandoned supplies. They also passed graves of people who had died from sickness, starvation, accidents, or bad weather.

The toughest part of the trip was crossing rivers and mountains. Even in good weather, this was challenging! So, the pioneers tried to cross them before winter set in.

Still, many wagons sunk or tipped in the rivers. And, others were **damaged** while being pulled over the Rocky Mountains with ropes and logs.

The Columbia River was a very dangerous crossing. It had fast rapids. It could take days for a wagon train to cross the river.

Following Landmarks

The land along the Oregon Trail was wild and unsettled. This made it easy to get lost!

Landmarks were like road signs. **Pioneers** used them to find their way. Landmarks also helped people know where they were on the trail.

Fur traders and mountain men named some of the trail's most famous landmarks. These include Chimney Rock, Independence Rock, and Soda Springs.

Chimney Rock looks like a tall chimney. This 325-foot (99-m) rock is located in Nebraska.

The Oregon Trail officially ended in Oregon City, Oregon. People rushed toward this last **landmark**. When it came into view, they knew their journey was almost complete. They would soon claim land and a new life!

Over the years, thousands of people traveled the Oregon Trail. Until 1914, some of them traveled the trail in wagons! Others took trains.

In time, the trip was made easier. In the 1860s, some people started to travel west on trains.

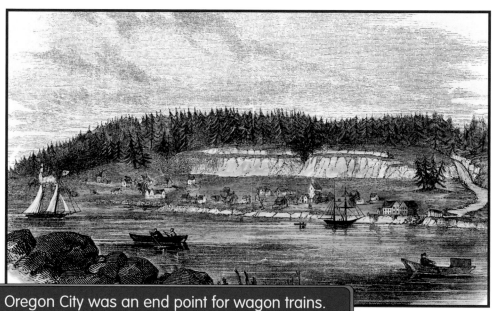

Oregon City was an end point for wagon trains. From there, many pioneers went their own way.

Detour ⬇

Did You Know?

. . . The Oregon Trail's halfway point was South Pass in the Rocky Mountains. Some pioneers went north to Oregon, while others went south toward California's gold.

. . . One famous mountain trail was Devil's Backbone. It was so narrow that wagons and people had to cross it in straight lines!

. . . Ezra Meeker is famous for traveling east on the Oregon Trail in 1902 when he was 76. He wanted people to remember the journey of the pioneers. So, he marked historic spots and raised money to help save the trail.

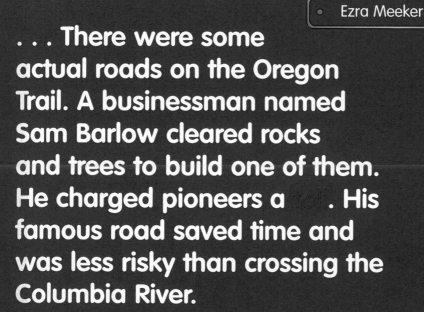

Ezra Meeker

. . . There were some actual roads on the Oregon Trail. A businessman named Sam Barlow cleared rocks and trees to build one of them. He charged pioneers a toll. His famous road saved time and was less risky than crossing the Columbia River.

The Oregon Trail Today

It is still possible to see the Oregon Trail and its **landmarks**. People can visit museums filled with **artifacts** from **pioneers**. Some **modern** families even **reenact** the wagon ride. And, children can play computer games to explore life on the Oregon Trail.

The last wagon crossed the trail in 1914. But, it is still possible to see some of the wagon ruts today!

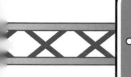
artifact an important object from history.

boosters people who encouraged others to move west. They described benefits, such as free land.

damage to cause injury or harm.

landmark a feature that is easily recognized.

modern relating to the present day.

pioneers people who traveled across the United States in the 1800s to settle the West.

reenact to act or perform the actions of an earlier event.

toll a charge to use something.

WEB SITES

To learn more about the Oregon Trail, visit ABDO Publishing Company on the World Wide Web. Web sites about the Oregon Trail are featured on our Book Links page. These links are routinely monitored and updated to provide the most current information available.
www.abdopublishing.com

Index